PRAYERS & TRUTHS TO ARMOR YOUR SOUL

VISION EXCHANGE, INC.

PO Box 35101
Elmwood Park, IL 60707
visionexchange.org

Written and compiled by Janet Back
Illustrated by Allen D. Warner

In accordance with c.827, permission to publish is granted on March 10, 2022, by Most Reverend Robert G. Casey, Vicar General of the Archdiocese of Chicago. Permission to publish is an official declaration of ecclesiastical authority that the material is free from doctrinal and moral error. No legal responsibility is assumed by the grant of this permission.

All Rights Reserved. No part of this publication may be reproduced or utilized in any form or by any means, electronic or mechanical, including photocopying, recording, or by any information storage and retrieval system, without prior permission in writing from the Publisher. Copyright ©2021 Vision Exchange Inc.

Request for information should be addressed to Vision Exchange, P.O. Box 35101, Elmwood Park, IL 60707 or visit www.visionexchange.org.

First Edition, 2022

Printed in the United States of America

Written and compiled by Janet Back.
Illustrated by Allen D. Warner

TABLE OF CONTENTS

1. **The Rosary**
   - How to Pray the Rosary 1-4
   - Mysteries of the Rosary 5-8
   - 15 Promises of the Rosary 9-10
2. **The Divine Mercy Chaplet**
   - How to Pray the Divine Mercy Chaplet 11-12
3. **A Prayer for Priests** 13
4. **Miraculous Medal Invocation** 13
5. **God Bless America** 13
6. **The Ten Commandments** 14
7. **The Beatitudes** 15
8. **Stations of the Cross** 16-19
9. **Key Prayers** 20
   - St. Michael the Archangel Prayer 20
   - Act of Contrition 20
   - Guardian Angel Prayer 20
   - Grace Before Meals 20
   - Grace After Meals 21
   - Act of Adoration and Reparation to Jesus 21
   - Memorare 21
   - Serenity Prayer 22
   - Ancient Prayer to St. Joseph 22
   - Prayer for Those Who Have Died 22
   - Prayer for a Holy Death 23
   - St. Gertrude the Great – Prayer for the Holy Souls 23
   - The Theological Virtues: Faith, Hope and Charity Prayers 23-24
   - The Four Cardinal Virtues 24-25
   - Virtues Versus Vices 26
   - Prayer to Pray for Virtues – Thomas Aquinas 27
   - Prayer for the Unborn 28
   - The Magnificat 28-30
   - St. Andrew Christmas Novena 31
10. **The Seven Gifts of the Holy Spirit** 32-34
11. **Twelve Fruits of the Holy Spirit** 35
12. **Come Holy Spirit Prayer** 35
13. **St. Augustine's Prayer to the Holy Spirit** 35

14. The Seven Sorrows and Joys of Our Lady 36
15. Prayer Before a Crucifix 36
16. The Seven Sacraments 37
17. The Seven Corporal Works of Mercy 37
18. The Seven Spiritual Works of Mercy 37
19. Eucharistic Exposition and Reposition Prayers 38-39
20. The Divine Praises 40
21. The Angelus 41
22. Driving Protection Prayers 41
23. Prayer for Purity to St. Joseph 42
24. Prayers from Great Saints 42
   - The Breastplate of St. Patrick 42
   - Prayer of St. Thomas Aquinas 42
   - Prayer of St. Francis of Assisi 43
   - Prayer of St. Benedict 44
   - Prayer of St. Dominic 44
   - St. Anthony Prayer 45
25. Our Lady of All Nations Prayer 45
26. Prayers of the Mass 46
   - The Confiteor 46
   - The Gloria 47
   - The Nicene Creed 48-49
   - The Sanctus 50
27. The Golden Arrow Prayer 50
28. 25 Secrets of Spiritual Warfare 51
29. Chaplet of St. Michael 52-54
30. First Saturday Invocations and Prayers 55
   - Fatima Sacrifice Prayer 55
   - Fatima Pardon Prayer 55
   - Fatima Angels Prayer 55
   - Fatima Eucharistic Prayer 55
   - Prayer to Our Lady of Fatima 56
   - Fatima Rosary Decade Prayer 56
31. Anima Christi Prayer 56
32. Act of Consecration to the Sacred Heart 57
33. Prayer to the Sacred Heart of Jesus 58
34. Prayer for Vocations – by St. Faustina 58
35. Padre Pio's Favorite Prayer of Petition 59
36. Flos Carmeli Prayer 60

HOW TO PRAY THE ROSARY

1. Make the Sign of the Cross and on the Crucifix – Pray: The Apostles Creed

Apostles Creed
I believe in God, the Father Almighty, Creator of Heaven and Earth
And in Jesus Christ, His only Son, Our Lord;
Who was conceived by the Holy Spirit, born of the Virgin Mary,
Suffered under Pontius Pilate, was crucified, died and was buried.
He descended into hell; and on the third day He arose again from the dead:
He ascended into heaven, and is seated at the right hand of God, the Father Almighty; from thence he shall come to judge the living and the dead.
I believe in the Holy Spirit, the Holy Catholic Church, the communion of saints,
The forgiveness of sins, the resurrection of the body, and life everlasting. Amen

2. On the first bead – Pray: The Our Father

Our Father
Our Father who art in Heaven
Hallowed be thy Name
Thy Kingdom come, Thy Will be done
On earth as it is in Heaven
Give us this Day, Our daily Bread
And forgive us our trespasses
As we forgive those who trespass against us
And lead us not into temptation
But deliver us from evil, Amen

3. On the next 3 beads – Pray: The Hail Mary (also known as the Angelic Salutation)

Hail Mary
Hail Mary Full of Grace
The Lord is with Thee
Blessed are Thou among women
And Blessed is the Fruit of Thy womb, Jesus
Holy Mary, Mother of God
Pray for us sinners, now and at the hour of our death, Amen

4. Pray: Glory Be (known as the Doxology - A short hymn like verse that praises the glory of God)

Glory Be
All Glory Be to the Father, and to the Son and to the Holy Spirit
As it was in the beginning, is now, and ever shall be world without end, Amen

5. Begin with the First Mystery (determined by day of the week)

MYSTERIES OF THE ROSARY
Joyful (Monday & Saturday)
1. Annunciation
2. Visitation of Mary with St. Elizabeth
3. Nativity of Our Lord
4. Presentation of Our Lord
5. Finding of Our Lord in the Temple

Luminous (Thursday)
1. Baptism of Jesus in the Jordan
2. Wedding Feast at Cana
3. Proclamation of the Kingdom of God & Call to Conversion
4. Transfiguration on the Mountain
5. Jesus gives us the Eucharist

Sorrowful (Tuesday & Friday)
1. Agony in the Garden
2. Scourging at the Pillar
3. Crowning of Thorns
4. Carry of the Cross
5. The Crucifixion

Glorious (Wednesday & Sunday)
1. Resurrection of Our Lord
2. Ascension of Our Lord into Heaven
3. Descent of the Holy Spirit
4. Assumption of the Blessed Virgin Mary into Heaven
5. Coronation of Mary, Queen of Heaven & Earth

6. Pray an Our Father
7. Pray 10 Hail Marys
8. Pray a Glory Be

9. Say the Prayer from Our Lady of Fatima

Our Lady of Fatima Rosary Decade Prayer:
Oh, my Jesus forgive us our sins, save us from the fires of hell, lead all souls to Heaven, especially those in most need of thy mercy.

10. Say the 2nd Mystery, 1 Our Father, 10 Hail Marys, a Glory Be, the Our Lady of Fatima prayer
11. Say the 3rd Mystery, 1 Our Father, 10 Hail Marys, a Glory Be, the Our Lady of Fatima prayer
12. Say the 4th Mystery, 1 Our Father, 10 Hail Marys, a Glory Be, the Our Lady of Fatima prayer
13. Say the 5th Mystery, 1 Our Father, 10 Hail Marys, a Glory Be, the Our Lady of Fatima prayer
14. Pray the Hail Holy Queen

Hail Holy Queen (also known as the Salve Regina)
Hail, Holy Queen, Mother of Mercy - Our life, our sweetness, and our Hope.
To thee do we cry, poor banished children of Eve:
To thee do we send up our sighs, mourning and weeping in this valley of tears.
Turn, then, O most gracious Advocate, thine eyes of mercy toward us:
And after this, our exile, show unto us the blessed fruit of thy womb, Jesus;
O clement, O loving, O sweet Virgin Mary.
Pray for us O Holy Mother of God
That we may be made worthy of the promises of Christ
Let us pray:
Oh God, whose only begotten Son, by His life, death, and resurrection,
Has purchased for us the rewards of Eternal life
Grant, we beseech thee, that while meditating upon these mysteries of the Most
Holy Rosary, of the Blessed Virgin Mary, we may imitate what they contain,

and obtain what they promise, through thy same Christ, Our Lord, Amen

15. Finally say: For the godly intentions of Our Holy Father: Then pray an Our Father, Hail Mary, And All Glory Be.

16. You can end with praying the **St. Michael the Archangel Prayer**

St. Michael the Archangel, defend us in battle, Be our protection against the wickedness and snares of the devil
May God rebuke him, we humbly pray, And do thou oh prince of the heavenly Host
By the Power of God
Cast into hell Satan, and all the evil spirits, who roam throughout the world seeking the ruin of souls - Amen.

Some people have added an additional prayer after the Our Lady of Fatima Rosary Decade Prayer, e.g. "Jesus protect and save the unborn".

THE JOYFUL MYSTERIES

THE ANNUNCIATION

THE VISITATION

NATIVITY OF OUR LORD

THE PRESENTATION

FINDING OF OUR LORD IN THE TEMPLE

THE LUMINOUS MYSTERIES

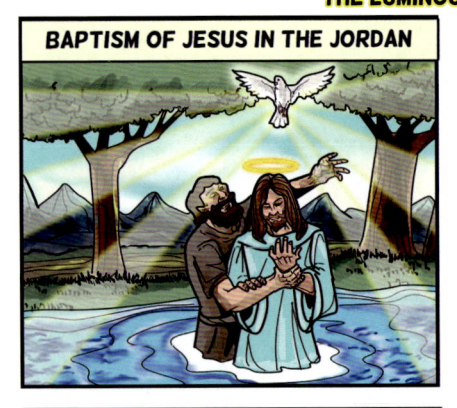

BAPTISM OF JESUS IN THE JORDAN

WEDDING FEAST AT CANA

PROCLAMATION OF THE KINGDOM OF GOD & CALL TO CONVERSION

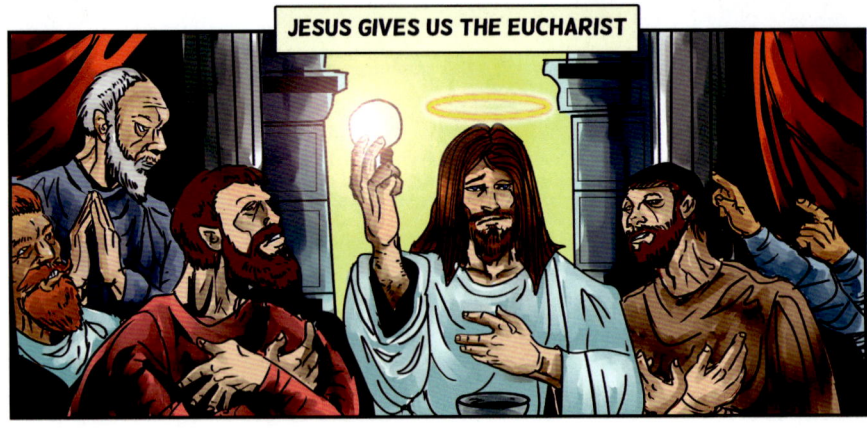

TRANSFIGURATION ON THE MOUNTAIN

JESUS GIVES US THE EUCHARIST

THE SORROWFUL MYSTERIES

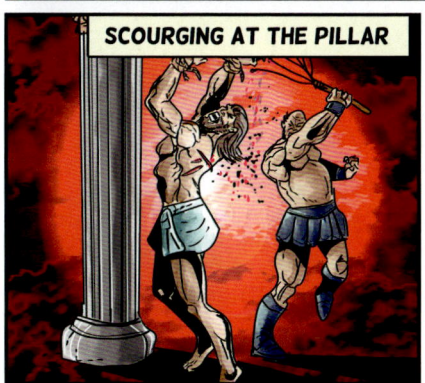

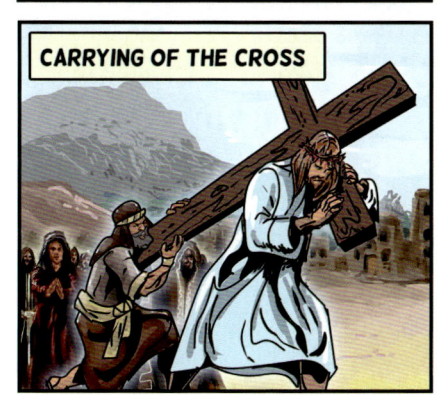

AGONY IN THE GARDEN

SCOURGING AT THE PILLAR

CROWNING OF THORNS

CARRYING OF THE CROSS

THE CRUCIFIXION

THE GLORIOUS MYSTERIES

RESURRECTION OF OUR LORD

ASCENSION OF OUR LORD INTO HEAVEN

DESCENT OF THE HOLY SPIRIT

ASSUMPTION OF THE BLESSED VIRGIN MARY INTO HEAVEN

CORONATION OF MARY, QUEEN OF HEAVEN & EARTH

15 PROMISES OF THE ROSARY

Given by Our Lady to St. Dominic & Bl. Alan de la Roche

1. Whosoever shall faithfully serve me by the recitation of the rosary shall receive signal graces.

2. I promise My special protection and the greatest graces to all those who shall recite the rosary.

3. The rosary shall be a powerful armor against Hell, it will destroy vice, decrease sin, and defeat heresies.

4. It will cause good works to flourish; it will obtain for souls the abundant mercy of God; it will withdraw the hearts of men (and women) from the love of the world and its vanities and will lift them to the desire for eternal things. Oh, that souls would sanctify themselves by this means.

5. The soul which recommends itself to me by the recitation of the Rosary shall not perish.

6. Whosoever shall recite the rosary devoutly, applying himself (herself) to the consideration of its sacred mysteries shall never be conquered by misfortune. God will not chastise him in His justice, he shall not perish by an unprovoked death; if he be just, he shall remain in the Grace of God, and become worthy of Eternal Life.

7. Whoever shall have true devotion for the rosary shall not die without the Sacraments of the Church.

8. Those who are faithful to recite the rosary shall have during their life and at their death, the Light of God and the plenitude of His graces; at the moment of death, they shall participate in the merits of the saints in Paradise.

9. I shall deliver from Purgatory those who have been devoted to the rosary.

10. The faithful children of the rosary shall merit a high degree of glory in Heaven.

11. You shall obtain all you ask of me by recitation of the rosary.

12. All those who propagate the Holy Rosary shall be aided by me in their necessities.

13. I have obtained from my Divine Son that all the advocates of the rosary shall have for intercessors the entire celestial court during their life and at the hour of death.

14. All who recite the rosary are my sons and daughters, and brothers and sisters of my only Son, Jesus Christ.

15. Devotion to my rosary is a great sign of predestination.[1]

HOW TO PRAY THE DIVINE MERCY CHAPLET

Diary, Saint Maria Faustina Kowalska, Divne Mercy in My Soul © 1987 (1209-1229; 476) Expanded Edition

1. Make the Sign of the Cross and Pray the Opening Prayer with a rosary:

"You expired, Jesus, but the source of Life gushed forth for souls, And the ocean of Mercy opened up for the whole world, O Fount of Life, Unfathomable Divine Mercy, envelop the whole world, and empty yourself upon us,

Oh, Blood and water which gushed forth from the heart of Jesus, as a fount of Mercy for us, I trust in You
Oh, Blood and water, which gushed forth from the heart of Jesus, as a fount of Mercy for us, I trust in You
Oh, Blood and water, which gushed forth from the heart of Jesus, as a fount of Mercy for us, I trust in You"

2. Pray an Our Father
3. Pray a Hail Mary
4. Pray the Apostles Creed

5. For the 1st decade Pray the "Eternal Father" Prayer:
   "Eternal Father, I offer You the Body and Blood, Soul and Divinity of Your dearly beloved Son, Our Lord Jesus Christ, in atonement for our sins and those of the whole world"

6. Then say 10 times:
   "For the sake of His Sorrowful Passion, have mercy on us and on the whole world"

7. For the 2nd decade repeat the "Eternal Father" Prayer
   Then repeat 10 times: "For the sake of His Sorrowful Passion, have mercy on us and on the whole world"
8. For the 3rd decade repeat the "Eternal Father" Prayer
   Then repeat 10 times: "For the sake of His Sorrowful Passion, have mercy on us and on the whole world"
9. For the 4th decade repeat the "Eternal Father" Prayer
   Then repeat 10 times: "For the sake of His Sorrowful Passion, have mercy on us and on the whole world"

10. For the 5th decade repeat the "Eternal Father" Prayer
    Then repeat 10 times: "For the sake of His Sorrowful Passion, mercy on us and on the whole world"

11. Pray 3 times: "Holy God, Holy Mighty One, Holy Immortal One, have mercy on us and on the whole world"

12. Then say: "Jesus I trust in You", "Jesus I trust in You", "Jesus I trust in You"

Closing Prayer:
"Eternal God, in whom mercy is endless, and the treasury of compassion inexhaustible, look kindly upon us, and increase Your mercy in us, that in difficult moments, we might not despair, nor become despondent, but with great confidence, submit ourselves to Your Holy Will, which is Love and Mercy Itself. Amen."

Afterwards say: "Saint Maria Faustina Pray for us"
End by saying five times: "My Jesus I love and venerate your sacred wounds, by whose merit I am redeemed" (This is said in honor of the five Sacred wounds of Jesus)

Our Lord said to St. Faustina:
> Encourage souls to say the chaplet which I have given you… Whoever will recite it will receive great mercy at the hour of death…. When they say this chaplet in the presence of the dying, I will stand between My Father and the dying person, not as the just Judge but as the merciful Savior. … Priests will recommend it to sinners as their last hope of salvation. Even if there were a sinner most hardened, if he were to recite this chaplet only once, he would receive grace from My infinite mercy. I desire to grant unimaginable graces to those souls who trust in My mercy. … Through the Chaplet you will obtain everything, if what you ask for is compatible with My will.[2] (Diary, 687, 1541, 1731)

A PRAYER FOR PRIESTS
BY ST. THERESE OF THE CHILD OF JESUS

O Jesus, I pray for Your faithful and fervent priests; for Your unfaithful and tepid priests; for Your priests laboring at home and abroad in distant mission fields; for Your tempted priests; for Your lonely and desolate priests; for Your young priests; for Your dying priests; for the souls of Your priests in purgatory. But above all I recommend to you the priests dearest to me; the priest who baptized me; the priests who absolved me from my sins; the priest at whose Masses I assisted and who gave me Your Body and Blood in Holy communion; the priests who taught and instructed me; all the priests to whom I am indebted in any other way. O Jesus, keep them close to your heart, and bless them abundantly in time and in eternity. Amen.

MIRACULOUS MEDAL INVOCATION
By St. Catherine Of Laboure

"Oh, Mary conceived without sin, pray for us who have recourse to thee."

The Family that Prays together Stays together!

GOD BLESS AMERICA
Peace Song Written by Irving Berlin in 1938

God bless America, land that I love
Stand beside her, and guide her
Through the night to the light from above.
From the mountains to the prairies
To the oceans white with foam.
God bless America
My home sweet home.

THE 10 COMMANDMENTS

The Commandments have been provided to us as Rules to follow during our life. However, the 10 Commandments are more than "Life Rules". By obeying them, you can avoid offending God and committing sin.

Remember, the 10 Commandments were written in stone, given to us directly from God to Moses on Mt. Sinai, and are meant to be followed. Since they come from God Himself, they are divine law. They are not 10 suggestions to be observed only when we feel like it. Rather, they are fundamentals for flourishing which God has given us to obey to ensure our earthly happiness and to guide us on the road to eternal happiness. Jesus states in Matthew 19:17, "If you wish to enter into life, keep the commandments."

1. "I am the Lord thy God, thou shalt not have any strange gods before Me."
2. "Thou shalt not take the name of the Lord thy God in vain."
3. "Remember to keep holy the Sabbath day."
4. "Honor thy father and mother."
5. "Thou shalt not kill."
6. "Thou shalt not commit adultery."
7. "Thou shalt not steal."
8. "Thou shalt not bear false witness against thy neighbor."
9. "Thou shalt not covet thy neighbor's wife."
10. "Thou shalt not covet thy neighbor's goods."

THE BEATITUDES

Jesus gave us the Beatitudes, or solemn blessings, during the Sermon on the Mount, teaching us ways that help us live like Christ. The Sermon on the Mount is the very first of Our Lord's sermons, and He teaches us how we should live, and what blessings will be granted to us in living in His Ways. They are found in the Gospel of St. Matthew (5:3-10) and four also appear in the Gospel of St. Luke (6:22)

- **Blessed are the poor in spirit, for theirs is the kingdom of heaven.**
- **Blessed are they who mourn, for they will be comforted.**
- **Blessed are the meek, for they will inherit the land.**
- **Blessed are they who hunger and thirst for righteousness, for they will be satisfied.**
- **Blessed are the merciful, for they will be shown mercy.**
- **Blessed are the clean of heart, for they will see God.**
- **Blessed are the peacemakers, for they will be called children of God.**
- **Blessed are they who are persecuted for the sake of righteousness, for theirs is the kingdom of heaven.**

STATIONS OF THE CROSS

1. Jesus is condemned to death
2. Jesus takes up His Cross
3. Jesus falls the first time
4. Jesus meets His Most Holy Mother
5. Simon of Cyrene helps Jesus carry His Cross
6. Veronica wipes the face of Jesus
7. Jesus falls a second time
8. Jesus speaks to the women of Jerusalem
9. Jesus falls the third time
10. Jesus is stripped of His Clothing
11. Jesus is nailed to the Cross
12. Jesus dies on the Cross
13. Jesus is taken down from the Cross
14. Jesus is laid in the sepulcher

Jesus is Risen from the Dead

After each Station, say: "We adore Thee Oh Christ and we praise Thee, because by thy Holy Cross, Thou has redeemed the world."

STATIONS OF THE CROSS

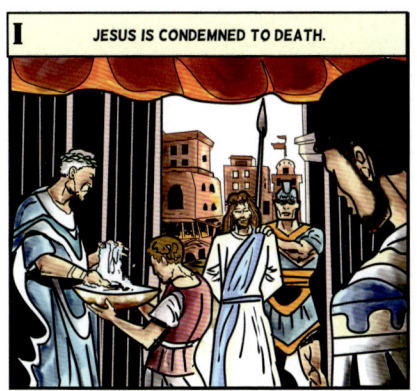

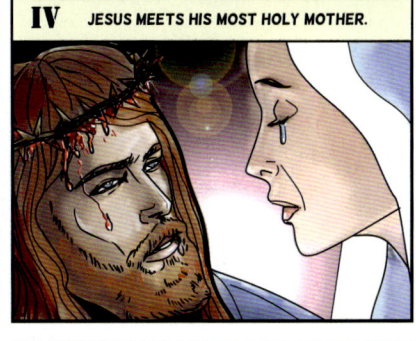

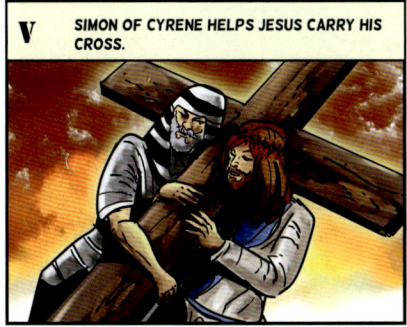

I — JESUS IS CONDEMNED TO DEATH.

II — JESUS TAKES UP HIS CROSS.

III — JESUS FALLS THE FIRST TIME.

IV — JESUS MEETS HIS MOST HOLY MOTHER.

V — SIMON OF CYRENE HELPS JESUS CARRY HIS CROSS.

VI — VERONICA WIPES THE FACE OF JESUS.

VII JESUS FALLS A SECOND TIME.	**VIII** JESUS SPEAKS TO THE WOMEN OF JERUSALEM.
IX JESUS FALLS THE THIRD TIME.	**X** JESUS IS STRIPPED OF HIS CLOTHING.
XI JESUS IS NAILED TO THE CROSS.	**XII** JESUS DIES ON THE CROSS.

| XIII | JESUS IS TAKEN DOWN FROM THE CROSS. |
| XIV | JESUS IS LAID IN THE SEPULCHER. |

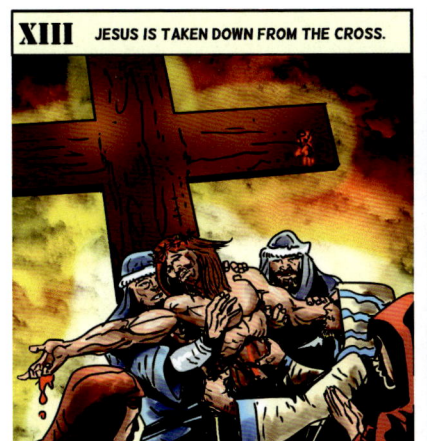

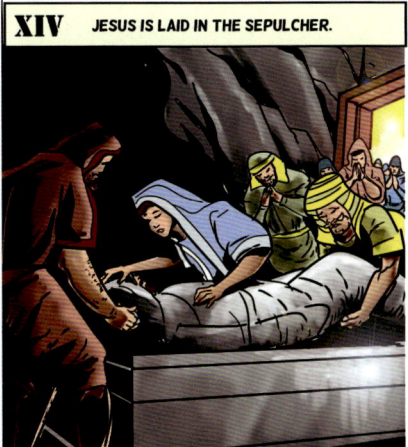

THE RESURRECTION !

KEY PRAYERS

ST. MICHAEL THE ARCHANGEL PRAYER

St. Michael the Archangel
Defend us in Battle
Be our Protection against the wickedness
and snares of the devil
May God rebuke him, we humbly pray
And do thou oh Prince of the Heavenly Host
By the Power of God
Cast into Hell satan and all the evil spirits
Who prowl throughout the world seeking the ruin of souls, Amen.

ACT OF CONTRITION

O my God, I am heartily sorry for having offended Thee, and I detest all my sins, because I dread the loss of Heaven and the pains of Hell, but most of all because they offend You, oh my God, Who art all-good and deserving of all my love. I firmly resolve, with the help of Thy grace, to confess my sins, do penance, and to amend my ways. Amen.

GUARDIAN ANGEL PRAYER

Angel of God, My Guardian Dear
To whom God's love, commits me here
Ever this Day/Night,
Be at my side
To Light and Guard
To Rule and Guide, Amen.

GRACE BEFORE MEALS

Bless us O Lord, and these Thy gifts,
Which we are about to receive, from Thy bounty,
Through Christ our Lord, Amen.

GRACE AFTER MEALS
We give Thee thanks, almighty God,
For all Thy blessings, which we have received
From Thy bounty, through Christ our Lord. Amen.

ACT OF ADORATION AND REPARATION TO JESUS IN THE BLESSED SACRAMENT
Oh, Sacrament Most Holy, Oh Sacrament Divine
All praise and all thanksgiving, be every moment thine.

MEMORARE
REMEMBER, O most gracious Virgin Mary,
that never was it known that anyone who fled to
thy protection, implored thy help, or sought thy intercession was left unaided.
Inspired by this confidence, I fly unto thee,
O Virgin of virgins, my Mother; to thee do I come;
before thee I stand, sinful and sorrowful.
O Mother of the Word Incarnate, despise not my petitions, but in thy mercy hear and answer me. Amen.

This is also known as the "**Emergency Novena**"
If you are in a situation you feel requires urgent prayers, simply pray this 9 times for help and 1 extra time in thanksgiving and Our Lady will be sure to intercede.

St. Bernard of Clairvaux is given credit for writing this powerful prayer. We ask Mary to be our Advocate, to take our petitions to Jesus, who we know, is more than happy to listen to His Mother's pleas on our behalf.

SERENITY PRAYER
God, grant me the serenity to accept the things I cannot change,
The courage to change the things I can,
And the wisdom to know the difference.

ANCIENT PRAYER TO ST. JOSEPH
Oh St. Joseph, whose protection is so great, so strong, so prompt before the throne of God,
I place in you all my interests and desires.
Oh St. Joseph, do assist me by your powerful intercession and obtain for me from your Divine Son all spiritual blessings through Jesus Christ, our Lord;
so that having engaged here below your Heavenly power, I may offer my thanksgiving and homage to the most loving of Fathers.
Oh St. Joseph, I never weary contemplating you and Jesus asleep in your arms.
I dare not approach while He reposes near your heart.
Press Him in my name and kiss His fine head for me,
and ask Him to return the kiss when I draw my dying breath.
St. Joseph, patron of departing souls, pray for me, Amen.

It has been said that whoever reads this prayer or hears it or carries it, will never die a sudden death, nor be drowned, nor will poison take effect on them. They will not fall into the hands of the enemy nor be burned in any fire, nor will they be defeated in battle. - [3]

PRAYER FOR THOSE WHO HAVE DIED
"May the souls of the faithful departed, through the mercy of God, rest in peace, Amen"

PRAYER TO ST. JOSEPH FOR A HOLY DEATH
Oh glorious St. Joseph, behold I choose thee today for my special patron in life and at the hour of my death.

Preserve and increase in me the spirit of prayer and fervor in the service of God. Remove far from me every kind of sin; obtain for me that my death may not come upon me unawares, but that I may have time to confess my sins sacramentally and to bewail them with a most perfect understanding and a most sincere and perfect contrition, in order that I may breathe forth my soul into the hands of Jesus and Mary. Amen.

ST. GERTRUDE THE GREAT - PRAYER FOR THE HOLY SOULS
Eternal Father, I offer you the most Precious Blood of Your Divine Son, Jesus, in union with the Masses said throughout the world today, for all the Holy Souls in Purgatory,
For sinners everywhere,
For sinners in the universal church,
Those in my own home and within my family, Amen.

St. Gertrude the Great lived during the 14th century. She began receiving heavenly visions at age 25. According to tradition, Our Lord appeared to her and told her if one prayed this prayer from the heart, 1000 souls would be released from Purgatory every time it was prayed! [4]

***** And the souls we help in Purgatory then become our advocates and pray for us! *****

THE THEOLOGICAL VIRTUES: FAITH, HOPE AND CHARITY
Faith – a Divine virtue by which we firmly believe the truths that God has revealed

Hope – a Divine virtue by which we firmly trust that God will give us eternal life and the means to obtain it

Charity – a Divine virtue by which we love God above all things for His own sake, and our neighbor as ourselves for the love of God - [5]

ACT OF FAITH, HOPE AND CHARITY PRAYERS

Act of Faith Prayer:
O my God, I firmly believe that Thou art one God in three Divine Persons, the Father, the Son, and the Holy Spirit:
I believe that Thy Divine Son became man, and died for our sins, and that He will come to judge the living and the dead.
I believe these and all the truths which the Holy Catholic Church teaches, because Thou hast revealed them, who can neither deceive nor be deceived. Amen.

Act of Hope Prayer
O my God, relying on Thine infinite goodness and promises,
I hope to obtain pardon of my sins,
The help of Thy grace, and life everlasting,
Through the merits of Jesus Christ, My Lord and Redeemer. Amen.

Act of Charity Prayer
O my God, I love Thee above all things,
With my whole heart and soul,
because Thou art all-good and worthy of all my love.
I love my neighbor as myself for the love of Thee.
I forgive all who have injured me,
And ask pardon of all whom I have injured. Amen. [6]

THE 4 CARDINAL VIRTUES: PRUDENCE, JUSTICE, FORTITUDE AND TEMPERANCE

A *virtue* is a habit or firm disposition which inclines a person to do good and avoid evil. It allows the person not only to perform good acts, but ensures the person gives only their best. Thus, one always desires to do good if one is virtuous.[7]

The word "Cardinal" is derived from the Latin *cardo*, meaning "hinge." Therefore, the virtues of: Prudence, Justice, Fortitude and Temperance are called "cardinal" because all other virtues "hinge" upon them.[8]

- **Prudence** uses reason as a way of governing and disciplining oneself. It is ranked as the first Cardinal Virtue by St. Thomas Aquinas because it is concerned with the intellect. Prudence allows us to judge properly whether something is right or wrong. Ignoring sound advice, or warnings from others, simply because their judgment doesn't agree with ours, causes one to be imprudent.

- **Justice** enables us to regulate our dealings with others. St. Thomas Aquinas ranks it second because it is concerned with the will and the idea of rights. Our upbringing, religion, piety, and gratitude, all play into how we decide what is just or not. Injustice occurs when we deprive someone of that which he is owed. Legal rights can never outweigh natural ones, i.e. Every human being has the right to life.

- **Fortitude** is ranked third by St. Thomas Aquinas as it has to do with bravery. It gives us courage to overcome fear and conquer obstacles, but it is always excercised in accordance with reason. While Prudence and Justice help us determine what needs to be done, fortitude gives us the strength to carry it out. It is one of the Gift's of the Holy Spirit, and gives us courage to defend our Faith, and resist temptation. Connected to fortitude are endurance, patience, and perseverance.

- **Temperance** curbs the pleasures and urges of the sensual appetite, using reason. It controls our desires and passions, so we learn restraint. A disordered desire for anything can have disastrous consequences, both physical and moral, but with Temperance, we are kept from excess. Temperance helps us determine what is and what is not appropriate, and how much we can act on our desires while having constraint. Related to temperance are continence, humility, and meekness.[9]

In AD 590, Pope Gregory articulated a list of the Seven Deadly Sins. To combat these vices, the Seven Virtues were compiled by Aurelius Clemens Prudentius, a Christian governor who died around AD 410. Practicing Virtues is said to protect one against temptations from the Seven Deadly Sins.[10]

Virtues versus Vices

Virtue

Chastity
Purity, abstinence

Temperance
Discipline, self-control

Charity
Benevolence, generosity, sacrifice

Diligence
Persistence, thoroughness, ethics

Patience
Forgiveness, mercy, stamina

Kindness
Gentleness, compassion

Humility
Humbleness, modesty, reverence

Vice

Lust
Passions, desirous

Gluttony
Excess, voraciousness

Greed
Avarice, selfishness

Sloth
Laziness, indolence

Wrath
Fury, anger, rage

Envy
Jealousy, covetousness

Pride
Arrogance, inflated ego

PRAYER TO PRAY FOR VIRTUES:
by Thomas Aquinas

O Almighty and all-knowing God,
without beginning or end,
who art the giver, preserver, and rewarder of all virtue:
Grant me to stand firm on the solid foundation of faith,
be protected by the invincible shield of hope,
and be adorned by the nuptial garment of charity;

Grant me by justice to obey thee,
by prudence to resist the crafts of the Devil,
by temperance to hold to moderation,
by fortitude to bear adversity with patience;

Grant that the goods that I have I may share liberally
with those who have not,
and the good that I do not have I may seek with humility
from those who have;

Grant that I may truly recognize
 the guilt of the evil I have done,
and bear with equanimity the punishments I have deserved;
that I may never lust after the goods of my neighbor,
but always give thanks to thee for all thy good gifts...

Plant in me, O Lord, all thy virtues,
that in divine matters I might be devout,
in human affairs wise,
and in the proper needs of the flesh onerous to no one...
And grant that I may never rush to do things hastily,
nor balk to do things demanding,
so that I neither yearn for things too soon,
nor desert things before they are finished. Amen.[11]

PRAYER FOR THE UNBORN   BY JANET BACK

Dear Lord,

It is with great urgency that I ask You to protect all babies whose mothers are contemplating abortion. Please keep them safe and touch their mother's hearts so they choose life for their little one. Help the mothers to know that You are the Creator of all life and have created their child for a purpose – a purpose You cannot achieve unless their child is born into this world.

Please help the mothers to turn to You and Trust in Your Providence. Lead them to a Crisis Pregnancy Center and help them find other resources that will give support in the care of their child. But above all, dispel these mother's fears so they welcome their babies into this world knowing their child is a true Gift from God. We ask this through Christ our Lord, Amen.

MAGNIFICAT:

My soul magnifies the Lord, and my spirit rejoices in God my Saviour;
Because he has regarded the lowliness of His handmaid; for, behold, henceforth all generations shall call me blessed;
Because he who is mighty has done great things for me, and holy is His name;
And His mercy is from generation to generation on those who fear Him.
He has shown might with His arm, He has scattered the proud in the conceit of their heart.
He has put down the mighty from their thrones and has exalted the lowly.
He has filled the hungry with good things, and the rich He has sent away empty.
He has given help to Israel, His servant, mindful of His mercy--
Even as he spoke to our fathers--to Abraham and to His posterity forever.

   This Prayer was proclaimed by the Blessed Virgin Mary after she arrived at the home of her cousin, St. Elizabeth. At Mary's arrival, the child in Elizabeth's womb, St. John the Baptist, leapt for joy. Elizabeth became filled with the Holy Spirit and realized Mary was pregnant with Jesus – the long-awaited Messiah. Sensing the great mysteries surrounding Mary, Elizabeth exclaims, *"Blessed art thou among women, and blessed is the fruit of thy womb. And whence is this to me, that the mother of my Lord should come to me? For behold as soon as the voice of thy salutation sounded in my ears, the infant in my womb leaped for joy. Blessed art thou that hast believed, because those things shall be accomplished that were spoken to thee by thy Lord."* Luke 1: 42-45

Mary then spoke the beautiful words we call the Magnificat.

Imagine! The first one to jump for joy at Mary's arrival, is an unborn baby (St. John the Baptist). He instantly lets his mother, St. Elizabeth, know Mary has arrived and is carrying the baby Jesus. Mary was not that far along in her pregnancy, and yet, one unborn baby (St. John the Baptist) leaps for joy to let his mother know they are in the presence of Jesus, and the Blessed Mother. Elizabeth then declares, "Blessed art thou among women and blessed is the fruit of thy womb." It is through the movements of a baby (St. John the Baptist) in his mother's womb, that mankind learns about the presence of Our Savior, who is in the womb of the Virgin Mother Mary.

Interestingly, an unborn baby is the first person to alert his mother (St. Elizabeth) about baby Jesus. It is incredible that two little unborn babies can sense one another, so much so, that St. John the Baptist, leapt for joy the moment he hears Mary's greeting, because he knows she is carrying Jesus. It is astounding to think a little unborn baby, knows Mary is pregnant with Jesus, and he lets the world know how utterly happy he is by his leaping in his mother's womb, because Jesus is with us, although not yet, born!

God wanted to send a powerful Pro-Life message to us: Unborn babies, from the moment of conception, are living and growing human beings, and they can sense things happening outside of the womb. Their life must be treasured, safeguarded, and considered a Gift, because they are given to us directly from God- the Creator of all Life, and these little babies lives must never be ended by abortion. Even if abortion is legal, morally, we do not, under any circumstances, have the right from God to destroy these most precious, innocent, defenseless babies growing in the womb because they are human beings, created in His image and likeness. God has a purpose for every single child He creates, and they are every bit as human as we are, during all stages of their development within the womb. We have no right whatsoever to end an unborn baby's life, because that ends God's plans for that child and breaks His 5th Commandment, "Thou shall not kill".

The Feast of the Visitation of the Blessed Virgin Mary is on May 31st.

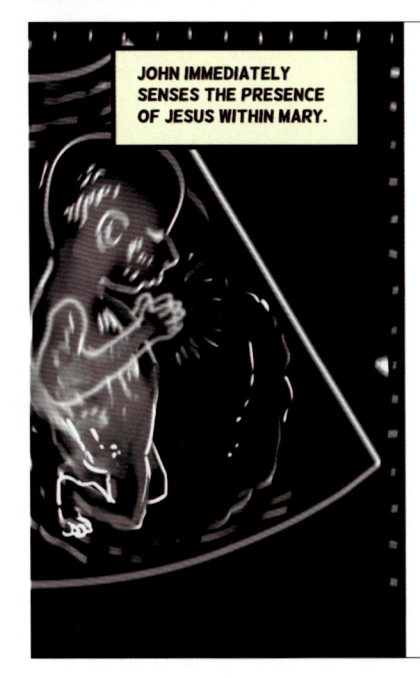

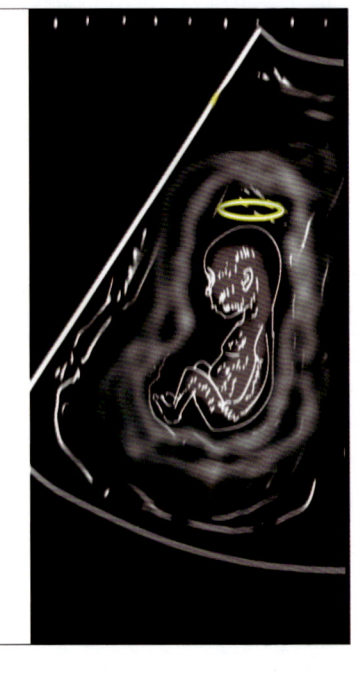

ST. ANDREW CHRISTMAS NOVENA

Hail and blessed be the hour and moment in which the Son of God was born of the most pure Virgin Mary, at midnight, in Bethlehem, in the piercing cold. In that hour vouchsafe, I beseech Thee, O my God, to hear my prayer and grant my desires through the merits of Our Savior Jesus Christ, and of His blessed Mother. Amen.

A Novena is prayed for 9 days, but this Novena Prayer is prayed much longer. It is prayed throughout Advent. While the origins of this prayer are unknown, it may have come from Ireland and is over 100 years old.

This Novena starts on St. Andrew's Feast Day, November 30th, and is prayed until December 24th. St. Andrew was the first disciple to be called by Jesus. He convinced his brother, Simon, to become a disciple of Jesus after exclaiming, "We have found the Messiah!". Simon became known as Peter and became the first Pope.

The prayer is to be said 15 times a day for 25 days, until Christmas Eve. This Novena prepares one's heart for the coming of Our Lord. It can be said at various time during the day, and does not need to be said all in one sitting. Ask the Lord for your petition, favor, request, or need, and it is believed whoever prays this Novena, will have their favor granted, if it is accordance to the Will of God.[12]

THE 7 GIFTS OF THE HOLY SPIRIT

- Wisdom
- Understanding
- Knowledge
- Fear of the Lord
- Counsel
- Fortitude
- Piety

Our Lord promised the apostles and disciples that He would send the Holy Spirit to be our Advocate before He ascended into Heaven. We pray the Holy Spirit gives us these Gifts. An explanation of each gift follows:

- **Spirit of Wisdom** - the ability and knowledge to make right choices in accordance with what God wants for us and to aspire to all things eternal
- **Spirit of Understanding** - the ability to grasp at the very heart of things, especially the teachings and mysteries of our Faith, and to be enlightened with higher truths God desires us to know
- **Spirit of Knowledge** - the ability to correctly judge the ways of the Lord so we take the right paths and grow in holiness
- **Spirit of Fear of the Lord** - the ability to continually revere God in all things and being afraid of separating ourselves from Him, while striving always to love Him above all else
- **Spirit of Counsel** - the ability to use right judgment in making choices so we follow the Will of God, especially in matters necessary for our salvation, and to avoid the deceits of the devil
- **Spirit of Fortitude** – the ability to have the courage to do what is right, and to be able to carry our cross, while overcoming obstacles jeopardizing our salvation because of our assurance of everlasting life
- **Spirit of Piety** – the ability to joyfully serve God and others, while ensuring worship, devotion, praise, and honor are dutifully given to Our Heavenly Father[13]

Frank Blisard writes eloquently about the Gifts of the Holy Spirit in an article in Catholic Answers. He states that according to St. Thomas Aquinas, these gifts provide "supernatural help" to grow in "perfection." With these Gifts, not only do we grow in perfection, but we grow in holiness so we can live the kind of life Christ envisioned for us. Aquinas emphasized the Gifts of the Holy Spirit are necessary for man's salvation, as we are unable to achieve salvation on our own. They will "perfect" the Four Cardinal Virtues (prudence, justice, fortitude, and temperance). However, it is the Theological virtue of Charity that unlocks the potential power of the Seven Gifts of the Holy Spirit. This virtue will remain inactive in the soul after baptism unless one begins to act in accordance with charity. Therefore, to embrace the power of the Seven Gifts of the Holy Spirit, it is best to be charitable with your time, talent, and treasure.

The Seven Gifts of the Holy Spirit work together with the: Cardinal and Theological Virtues, the Twelve Fruits of the Holy Spirit, and the Eight Beatitudes. By practicing the Cardinal and Theological Virtues, one begins to see an emergence of the Gifts of the Holy Spirit in one's life. When the Gifts of the Holy Spirit are effectively used, they produce the Fruits of the Holy Spirit: love, joy, peace, patience, kindness, goodness, generosity, faithfulness, gentleness, modesty, self-control, and chastity (Gal. 5:22–23).

Cooperation among Virtues, Gifts, and Fruits allows one to achieve the fulfillment of the Beatitudes, which Jesus stated in the Sermon on the Mount and are the ways in which He wants us to live. (Matt. 5:3–10).[14]

It is recommended we pray the Novena to the Holy Spirit during the Easter season, especially before Pentecost. It is the oldest of all Novenas. It was first made at the command of our Lord to His apostles as they waited in the upper room for the coming of the Holy Spirit on the first Pentecost. It is a powerful plea for light, strength and love needed by every Christian.

THE HOLY SPIRIT IS CALLED UPON DURING CONFIRMATION TO BRING FORTH HIS GIFTS OF:

Wisdom, Understanding, Knowledge, Fear of the Lord, Counsel, Fortitude and Piety, which enrich the candidate. The Sacrament of Confirmation "increases the Gifts of the Holy Spirit within us" (Catechism 1303). When the candidates, enriched with the Gifts of the Holy Spirit, cooperate with the graces the Holy Spirit provides, they can bear many Good Fruits of the Holy Spirit and, are more likely, and willing, to listen and obey the promptings of the Spirit.

The Good Fruits brought about by cooperating with the Holy Spirit are called Fruits of the Holy Spirit for a reason. We are the branches, connected to the Vine- who is Jesus. By staying attached to the Vine-Jesus, and by receiving nourishment from the Vine-the Eucharist, we, the branches, can cooperate with the Holy Spirit's promptings, thus bearing Good Fruit. If we detach ourselves from the Vine, sadly, rotten fruit develops from our broken branches. Therefore, keeping our branches pruned, through the Sacrament of Reconciliation, and receiving the necessary food-the Word of God & the Eucharist, ensures we bear Good Fruit.

THERE ARE 12 FRUITS OF THE HOLY SPIRIT

They will not only benefit us, but they will benefit and enrich others and the Church!

The 12 Traditional Fruits of the Holy Spirit

- **Charity**
- **Joy**
- **Peace**
- **Patience**
- **Kindness**
- **Goodness**
- **Generosity**
- **Gentleness/Humility**
- **Faithfulness**
- **Modesty**
- **Self-control**
- **Chastity** [15]

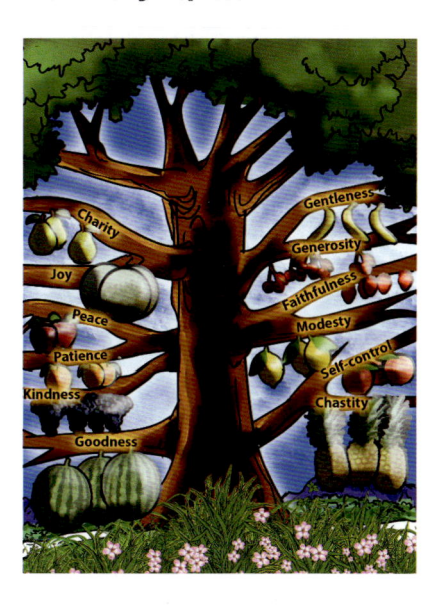

COME, HOLY SPIRIT

Come Holy Spirit, and fill the hearts of your faithful, and kindle in them the fire of Your Divine Love. Send forth Your Spirit and they shall be created, and You shall renew the face of the earth. Oh God, who by the light of the Holy Spirit instructed the hearts of the faithful, grant, that by the same Spirit we may be truly wise and ever rejoice in His consolation. We ask this through Christ Our Lord. Amen.

ST. AUGUSTINE'S PRAYER TO THE HOLY SPIRIT

Breathe in me, O Holy Spirit, that my thoughts may all be holy. Act in me, O Holy Spirit, that my work, too, may be holy. Draw my heart, O Holy Spirit, that I love but what is holy. Strengthen me, O Holy Spirit, to defend all that is holy. Guard me, then, O Holy Spirit, that I always may be holy. Amen.

THE 7 SORROWS (DOLORS) AND 7 JOYS OF OUR LADY

SORROWS (DOLORS)

1. The Prophecy of Simeon (Luke 2:33-35)
2. The Flight into Egypt (Matthew 3: 13-15)
3. Jesus is lost in the Temple (Luke 2: 41-52)
4. Jesus & Mary meet -Way of the Cross (John 19:17)
5. The Crucifixion of Our Lord (John 19: 25-30)
6. Jesus is taken down from the Cross (John 19: 31-37)
7. Jesus is laid in the Tomb (John 19:38-42)

JOYS:

1. The Annunciation (Luke 1:27-38)
2. The Visitation (Luke 1:39-58)
3. The Nativity of Our Lord (Luke 2:7)
4. The Magi Adore Jesus (Matthew 2: 7-11)
5. Finding Jesus in the Temple (Luke 2: 46)
6. The Resurrection (John 20:1-9)
7. Assumption & Coronation of Our Lady (Apocalypse 12)

PRAYER BEFORE A CRUCIFIX

Look down upon me, good and gentle Jesus,
while before Thy face
I humbly kneel and, with burning soul, pray and beseech Thee to
fix deep in my heart lively sentiments of faith, hope and charity;
true contrition for my sins, and a firm purpose of amendment.
While I contemplate, with great love and tender pity,
Thy five most precious wounds, pondering over them within me
and calling to mind thy words which David, thy prophet, said of Thee,
my Jesus:

"They have pierced My hands and My feet;
they have numbered all My bones"

THE 7 SACRAMENTS

1. **Baptism**
2. **Penance (Confession, Reconciliation)**
3. **Eucharist (Holy Communion)**
4. **Confirmation (Chrismation)**
5. **Matrimony**
6. **Holy Orders**
7. **Extreme Unction (Anointing of the Sick)**

There are Seven Sacraments. "A sacrament is an outward sign instituted by Christ to give grace." [16] Each of the sacraments also give a special grace, called <u>Sacramental Grace</u>. Think of the sacraments as streams of grace flowing from the Cross, through the Catholic Church, giving us: new life within our soul, God's guidance, the ability to make good choices versus bad, and what path to take so we can achieve eternity with Our Lord.[17]

We receive grace through the Sacraments and prayer. Grace is a gift given to us from God. Grace makes one's soul holy and beautiful, giving us a New Life in Christ. This New Life is called <u>Sanctifying Grace</u>, which comes to us from the Holy Spirit. We also can receive direct help from God through prayer, which is called <u>Actual Grace</u>. This Actual Help comes to us in the way of light for our mind and strength for our will, so we do what is right in the eyes of the Lord. Without grace one cannot save one's soul, but thankfully, through prayer and the Sacraments, God gives us an abundance of Sacramental, Sanctifying and Actual Grace.[18]

THE 7 CORPORAL WORKS OF MERCY

- To feed the hungry
- To give drink to the thirsty
- To clothe the naked
- To shelter the homeless
- To visit the sick
- To visit the imprisoned
- To bury the dead

THE 7 SPIRITUAL WORKS OF MERCY

- To counsel the doubtful
- To instruct the ignorant
- To admonish the sinner
- To comfort the sorrowful
- To forgive all injuries
- To bear wrongs patiently
- To pray for the living and the dead

EUCHARISTIC EXPOSITION AND BENEDICTION / REPOSITION OF THE BLESSED SACRAMENT

Stand: The altar server and presider enter the chapel. The presider carries the Luna with the Consecrated Host. A selected song is sung relating to the liturgical season or the mystery of the Eucharist.

Kneel: The presider places the Luna with the Consecrated Host into the monstrance. Once the presider has reached the front of the altar and kneels, he will lead all in singing the Salutaris or some other appropriate Eucharistic song.

O SAVING VICTIM

O saving Victim, opening wide
The gate of heaven to us below.
Our foes press on from every side;
Thine aid supply, thy strength bestow.

To your great name be endless praise,
Immortal Godhead, One in Three;
Grant us, for endless length of days,
In our true native land to be. Amen.

O SALUTARIS HOSTIA

O salutaris Hostia,
Quae caeli pandis ostium:
Bella premunt hostilia,
Da robur, fer auxilium

Uni trinoque Domino
Sit sempiterna gloria,
Qui vitam sine termino
Nobis donet in patria. Amen.

BENEDICTION OF THE BLESSED SACRAMENT

Kneel: Once Adoration is completed for the hour; the presider and altar server return to the front of the altar. While the presider incenses the monstrance, all sing the Tantum Ergo (or another appropriate Eucharistic song)

TANTUM ERGO

Down in adoration falling
To the everlasting Father,
Lo, the sacred host we hail;
And the Son who reigns on high,
Lo, o'er ancient forms departing,
With the Spirit blest proceeding
Newer rites of grace prevail;
Forth from each eternally,
Faith for all defects supplying,
Be salvation, honor, blessing,
Where the feeble senses fail.
Might, and endless majesty.
Amen

TANTUM ERGO

Tantum ergo Sacramentum
Veneremur cernui
Et antiquum documentum
Novo cedat ritui
Praestet fides supplementum
Sensuum defectui
Genitori, Genitoque
Laus et jubilatio
Salus, honor, virtus quoque
Sit et benedictio
Procedenti ab utroque
Compar sit laudatio. Amen

All remain kneeling when the Presider says, "Let us pray": Lord our God, you have given us the True Bread from Heaven

Response: "Having all sweetness within it"

All remain kneeling while the Presider makes the sign of the cross with the monstrance. All gathered then recite the Divine Praises.[19]

THE DIVINE PRAISES

Said during Benediction

Blessed be God.
Blessed be His Holy Name.
Blessed be Jesus Christ, true God and true man.
Blessed be the Name of Jesus.
Blessed be His Most Sacred Heart.
Blessed be His Most Precious Blood
Blessed be Jesus in the Most Holy Sacrament of the Altar.
Blessed be the Holy Spirit, the Paraclete.
Blessed be the great Mother of God, Mary most holy.
Blessed be her holy and Immaculate Conception.
Blessed be her glorious Assumption.
Blessed be the name of Mary, Virgin and Mother.
Blessed be St. Joseph, her most chaste spouse.
Blessed be God in His angels and in His saints.

May the heart of Jesus, in the Most Blessed Sacrament, be praised, adored, and loved with grateful affection, at every moment, in all the tabernacles of the world, even to the end of time. Amen.

THE ANGELUS

V. The Angel of the Lord declared unto Mary.
R. And she conceived of the Holy Spirit.
Hail Mary, full of grace,
The Lord is with Thee;
Blessed art thou among women,
And blessed is the fruit of thy womb, Jesus.
Holy Mary, Mother of God,
Pray for us sinners,
Now and at the hour of our death. Amen
V. Behold the handmaid of the Lord.
R. Be it done unto me according to thy word.
Hail Mary, etc.
V. And the Word was made Flesh.
R. And dwelt among us.
Hail Mary, etc.
V. Pray for us, O holy Mother of God.
R. That we may be made worthy of the promises of Christ.
LET US PRAY
Pour forth, we beseech Thee, O Lord, Thy grace into our hearts, that we to whom the Incarnation of Christ Thy Son was made known by the message of an angel, may by His Passion and Cross be brought to the glory of His Resurrection. Through the same Christ Our Lord. Amen.

DRIVING PROTECTION PRAYERS

1. Our Lady of the Highway (to be said, even if you are on the side streets)

"Our Lady of the Highway, pray for us (or protect us)."

2. Prayer to Saint Christopher

Grant me, O Lord, a steady hand and watchful eye.
That no one shall be hurt as I pass by.
You gave life, I pray no act of mine may take away or mar that gift of thine.
Shelter those, dear Lord, who bear my company, from the evils of fire and all calamity.
Teach me, to use my car for others need; Nor miss through love of undue speed The beauty of the world; that thus I may with joy and courtesy go on my way.
St. Christopher, holy patron of travelers, protect me and lead me safely to my destiny.

Prayer for Purity to St. Joseph

Oh, Guardian of Virgin and holy Father St. Joseph,
into whose faithful keeping were entrusted Christ Jesus,
Innocence itself,
and Mary, Virgin of virgins,
I pray and beseech thee by these dear pledges, Jesus and Mary,
that, being preserved from all uncleanness,
I may with spotless mind, pure heart and chaste body
ever serve Jesus and Mary most chastely all the days of my life.
Amen.

From "The Breastplate of St. Patrick"

Christ be with me, Christ within me,
Christ behind me, Christ before me,
Christ beside me, Christ to win me,
Christ to comfort and restore me.
Christ beneath me, Christ above me,
Christ in quiet, Christ in danger,
Christ in hearts of all that love me,
Christ in mouth of friend and stranger.

Prayer of St. Thomas Aquinas

Lord, Father all-powerful and ever-living God, I thank You, for
even though I am a sinner, your unprofitable servant, not
because of my worth but in the kindness of your mercy,
You have fed me with the Precious Body and Blood of Your Son,
our Lord Jesus Christ.
I pray that this Holy Communion may not bring me
condemnation and punishment but forgiveness and salvation.
May it be a helmet of faith and a shield of good will.
May it purify me from evil ways and put an end to my evil passions.
May it bring me charity and patience, humility and obedience,

and growth in the power to do good.
May it be my strong defense against all my enemies, visible and invisible, and the perfect calming of all my evil impulses,
bodily and spiritual.
May it unite me more closely to you, the One true God, and lead me
safely through death to everlasting happiness with You.
And I pray that You will lead me, a sinner, to the banquet where you,
with Your Son and Holy Spirit, are true and perfect light, total fulfillment, everlasting joy, gladness without end, and perfect happiness to your saints. Grant this through Christ our Lord. Amen.

Prayer of St. Francis of Assisi

This prayer was not written by St. Francis but appeared on a Holy Card with St. Francis' image in 1915 during WWI to pray for peace. [20]

Lord, make me an instrument of your peace.
Where there is hatred, let me sow love.
Where there is injury, pardon.
Where there is doubt, faith.
Where there is despair, hope.
Where there is darkness, light.
Where there is sadness, joy.
O Divine Master,
grant that I may not so much seek
to be consoled, as to console;
to be understood, as to understand;
to be loved, as to love.
For it is in giving that we receive.
It is in pardoning that we are pardoned,
and it is in dying that we are born to Eternal Life.

Prayer of St. Benedict

Gracious and holy Father,
grant us the intellect to understand you,
reason to discern you, diligence to seek you,
wisdom to find you, a spirit to know you,
a heart to meditate upon you.
May our ears hear you, may our eyes behold you,
and may our tongues proclaim you.
Give us grace that our way of life may be pleasing to you,
that we may have the patience to wait for you
and the perseverance to look for you.
Grant us a perfect end–your holy presence,
a blessed resurrection and life everlasting.
We ask this through Jesus Christ our Lord. Amen.

Prayer of St. Dominic

May God the Father who made us bless us.
May God the Son send his healing among us.
May God the Holy Spirit move within us and
give us eyes to see with, ears to hear with,
and hands that your work might be done.
May we walk and preach the word of
God to all.
May the angel of
peace watch over us
and
lead us at last by
God's grace to the
Kingdom. Amen.

Saint Anthony Prayer

O Holy St. Anthony, gentlest of saints, your love for God and Charity for His creatures, made you worthy, when on earth, to possess miraculous powers. Encouraged by this thought, I implore you to obtain for me (request). O gentle and loving St. Anthony, whose heart was ever full of human sympathy, whisper my petition into the ears of the sweet Infant Jesus, who loved to be folded in your arms; and the gratitude of my heart will ever be yours. Amen

OUR LADY OF ALL NATIONS PRAYER

Lord Jesus Christ
Son of the Father
Send now Your Spirit over the earth.
Let the Holy Spirit live in the hearts of all nations,
that they may be preserved from degeneration, disaster and war.
May the Lady of All Nations,
The Blessed Virgin Mary,
Be our Advocate.
Amen.
Imprimatur: +Jozef Punt, Haarlem-Amsterdam, 06.01.2009

PRAYERS OF THE MASS

The Confiteor

The Confiteor (it means, "I confess") is a general confession of sins. During this part of the Mass, we can ask God to forgive our venial sins we have committed. Venial sins weaken our relationship with God, while mortal sin breaks that relationship. For the forgiveness of mortal sins, we must go to confession, but for the venial sins, we can receive forgiveness during Mass by receiving Communion with contrition. However, we must prepare ahead of time, and think about our shortcomings for this confession of our venial sins to be effective. When we pray the Confiteor, we are asking God to forgive us for the bad things we have thought, said, and done, and the good we failed to do. However, we must have true contrition for our sins, and know what sins are weighing on our soul.[21]

During the early days of the Church, the Confiteor was probably a prayer said in private by the priest before he began Mass. According to the writings from the "Sixth Roman Ordo" we can ascertain that the Confiteor was established and became part of the Mass by the 11th century.[22]

I confess to almighty God and to you,
My brothers and sisters,
That I have greatly sinned,
In my thoughts and in my words,
In what I have done and in what I have failed to do,
(STRIKE CHEST 3 TIMES DURING THIS PART)
*Through my fault, through my fault,
Through my most grievous fault;*

therefore, I ask blessed Mary ever-Virgin,
And all the Angels and Saints,
And you, my brothers and sisters,
To pray for me to the Lord our God.

The Gloria

The Gloria is sung on Sundays, solemnities and feast days, except during Advent and Lent. It is called "the Angelic Hymn", since Heavenly Angels sang it proclaiming the Birth of Our Lord. In the Gospel of Luke 2:15, he writes that the angels sang, "Glory to God in the highest, and peace on earth to people of good will". This song glorifies God, asks for the mercy of Jesus, and finally acknowledges the mystery of the Trinity.[23]

This prayer dates back from the 6th century and was only used when a bishop was the celebrant on solemn feasts. Slowly priests began to use it, but only for Easter. Then, by the 12th century, it was in regular use at every Mass.[24]

Glory to God in the highest,
And on earth peace to people of good will.
We praise You, we bless You,
We adore You, we glorify You,
We give you thanks for your great glory,
Lord God, heavenly King,
O God, almighty Father.
Lord Jesus Christ, Only Begotten son,
Lord God, Lamb of God,
Son of the Father,
You take away the sins of the world,
Have mercy on us.
For you alone are the Holy One,
You alone are the Lord,
You alone are the Most High,
Jesus Christ,
With the Holy Spirit,
In the glory of God the Father – Amen

Nicene Creed

The Nicene Creed was written at the Councils of Nicaea (AD325) and later it was expanded to define the divinity of the Holy Spirit at Constantinople (AD381). It is also called the Niceno-Constantinopolitan Creed. In AD325, 318 bishops came from around the world in the 4th century to write the Creed. They presented the basic Catholic teaching about the nature of God. They wrote it because Arianism was spreading, which denied Jesus is fully divine. Several bishops were in attendance, who later became saints, including St. Silvester, St. Nicholas of Myra, St. Eusebius of Caesarea, St. Athanasius, and St. Alexander of Alexandria.[25]

The Creed explains the Church's teaching about the Trinity, and expresses historical facts about Jesus' life. While it does not quote Scripture, it is based on biblical truths.[26] Catholics, Orthodox, and many Protestants accept the ancient Nicene Creed. It became part of the Mass in the 6th century.

THE NICENE CREED

I believe in one God,
the Father Almighty,
Maker of heaven and earth,
of all things visible and invisible.
I believe in one Lord Jesus Christ,
the only-begotten Son of God,
born of the Father before all ages,
God from God, Light from Light,
true God from true God,
begotten, not made,
consubstantial with the Father.
Through him all things were made.
For us men and for our salvation
he came down from heaven,

Please bow for these words:
*and by the Holy Spirit was incarnate of the Virgin Mary,
and became man.*

For our sake he was crucified under Pontius Pilate;
he suffered death and was buried,
and rose again on the third day
in accordance with the Scriptures.
He ascended into heaven
and is seated at the right hand of the Father.
He will come again in glory to judge the living and the dead,
and his kingdom will have no end.
I believe in the Holy Spirit, the Lord, the giver of life,
who proceeds from the Father and the Son.
who with the Father and the Son he is adored and glorified.
who has spoken through the Prophets.
I believe in one, holy, catholic and apostolic Church.
I confess one baptism for the forgiveness of sins,
and I look forward to the resurrection of the dead,
and the life of the world to come. Amen.

THE SANCTUS

The Sanctus (Holy, Holy, Holy - is the Communion Part of the Mass) is inspired by two visions in the Bible. One is from Isaiah's vision of God's glory (Isaiah 6:3), and the other is from the vision of Heaven in John's Revelation (Revelation 4). It also includes a phrase from the Gospel said on Palm Sunday, "Blessed is he who comes in the name of the Lord. Hosanna in the highest" (Matthew 21:9).[27]

It is very ancient and may have come from prayers from the Jewish Faith. Pope St. Clement wrote a letter to the Corinthians (A.D. 88-97) and suggested the Sanctus was used by Christians. However, it was probably introduced to the Mass in the 3rd century. By saying, "God is the Lord of Hosts", we are proclaiming God is the Lord of the Angelic Choirs and the whole multitude of created beings, therefore it considers that the whole of creation is united in singing God's glory.[28]

Holy, Holy, Holy Lord God of hosts.
Heaven and earth are full of your glory.
Hosanna in the highest.
Blessed is he who comes in the name of the Lord.
Hosanna in the highest.

THE GOLDEN ARROW PRAYER

May the most holy, most sacred, most adorable, most incomprehensible and ineffable Name of God be forever praised, blessed, loved, adored, and glorified in Heaven, on earth, and under the earth, by all the creatures of God, and by the Sacred Heart of Our Lord Jesus Christ, in the Most Holy Sacrament of the Altar. **Amen.**

"The Golden Arrow" is a prayer for the reparation of Blasphemy against Jesus' Holy Name. Our Lord told Sister Marie of Saint Peter in August of 1843 in France, that "The Golden Arrow" prayer, dictated by Jesus, to Sister Marie, would delight Him, and he would be happy with those who recited this prayer. In addition, it would also heal those other wounds inflicted on Him by the malice of sinners. [29]

25 SECRETS OF SPIRITUAL WARFARE REVEALED TO US BY CHRIST TO SAINT FAUSTINA

1. Never trust in yourself but abandon yourself totally to My will.
2. In desolation, darkness and various doubts, have recourse to Me and to your spiritual director. He will always answer you in my name.
3. Do not bargain with any temptation; lock yourself immediately in My Heart.
4. At the first opportunity, reveal the temptation to the confessor.
5. Put your self-love in the last place, so that it does not taint your deeds.
6. Bear with yourself with great patience.
7. Do not neglect interior mortifications.
8. Always justify to yourself the opinions of your superiors and of your confessor.
9. Shun murmurs like a plague.
10. Let all act as they like; you are to act, as I want you to.
11. Observe the rule as faithfully as you can.
12. If someone causes you trouble, think what good you can do for the person who caused you to suffer.
13. Do not pour out your feelings.
14. Be silent when you are rebuked.
15. Do not ask everyone's opinion, but only the opinion of your confessor; be as frank and simple as a child with him.
16. Do not become discouraged by ingratitude.
17. Do not examine with curiosity the roads down which I lead you.
18. When boredom and discouragement beat against your heart, run away from yourself and hide in My heart.
19. Do not fear struggle; courage itself often intimidates temptations, and they dare not attack us.
20. Always fight with the deep conviction that I am with you.
21. Do not be guided by feeling, because it is not always under your control; but all merit lies in the will.
22. Always depend upon your superiors, even in the smallest things.
23. I will not delude you with prospects of peace and consolations; on the contrary, prepare for great battles.
24. Know that you are on a great stage where all of heaven and earth are watching you.
25. Fight like a knight, so I can reward you. Do not be unduly fearful, because you are not alone. [30] (Diary, 625)

CHAPLET OF ST. MICHAEL

Saint Michael the Archangel appeared one day to Antonia d'Astonac, a very devout and holy woman. St. Michael told her he wished to be honored by nine salutations corresponding to the nine Choirs of Angels, which should consist of one Our Father and three Hail Mary's in honor of each of the angelic choirs.

PROMISES OF ST. MICHAEL

Saint Michael the Archangel said that whoever would practice this devotion in his honor, before receiving Holy Communion, would be given an escort of nine angels chosen from each one of the nine Choirs of Angels. In addition, if one would pray these nine salutations daily, St. Michael promised his continual assistance and that of all the holy angels during one's life, and, after death, deliverance from purgatory for themselves and their relations.

HOW TO PRAY THE CHAPLET OF SAINT MICHAEL:

- Pray an Act of Contrition (page 20)
- Say "O God, come to my assistance. Make haste to help me."
- Pray one Glory Be
- Pray each salutation and afterwards pray one Our Father and three Hail Marys.

1. By the intercession of Saint Michael and the celestial Choir of Seraphim, may the Lord make us worthy to burn with the fire of perfect charity. Amen.

    Our Father……..Hail Mary…….Hail Mary…….Hail Mary……

2. By the intercession of Saint Michael and the celestial Choir of Cherubim, may the Lord vouchsafe to grant us grace to leave the ways of wickedness to run in the paths of Christian perfection. Amen.

    Our Father……..Hail Mary…….Hail Mary…….Hail Mary……

3. By the intercession of Saint Michael and the celestial Choir of Thrones, may the Lord infuse into our hearts a true and sincere spirit of humility. Amen.

    Our Father……..Hail Mary…….Hail Mary…….Hail Mary……

4. By the intercession of Saint Michael and the celestial choir of Dominions, may the Lord give us grace to govern our senses and subdue our unruly passions. Amen.

   Our Father........Hail Mary.......Hail Mary.......Hail Mary......

5. By the intercession of Saint Michael and the celestial Choir of Powers, may the Lord vouchsafe to protect our souls against the snares of temptations of the devil. Amen.

   Our Father........Hail Mary.......Hail Mary.......Hail Mary......

6. By the intercession of Saint Michael and the celestial Choir of Virtues, may the Lord preserve us from evil and suffer us not to fall into temptation. Amen.

   Our Father........Hail Mary.......Hail Mary.......Hail Mary......

7. By the intercession of Saint Michael and the celestial Choir of Principalities, may God fill our souls with a true spirit of obedience. Amen.

   Our Father........Hail Mary.......Hail Mary.......Hail Mary......

8. By the intercession of Saint Michael and the celestial Choir of Archangels, may the Lord give us perseverance in faith and in all good works, in order that we gain the glory of paradise. Amen.

   Our Father........Hail Mary.......Hail Mary.......Hail Mary......

9. By the intercession of Saint Michael and the celestial Choir of Angels, may the Lord grant us to be protected by them in this mortal life and conducted hereafter to eternal glory. Amen.

   Our Father........Hail Mary.......Hail Mary.......Hail Mary......

- Then say one Our Father in honor of Saint Michael,
  one Our Father in honor of Saint Gabriel,
  one Our Father in honor of Saint Raphael,
  one Our Father in honor of your Guardian Angel.

THE CHAPLET IS CONCLUDED WITH THE FOLLOWING PRAYERS:

O glorious Prince St. Michael, chief and commander of the heavenly hosts, guardian of souls, vanquisher of rebel spirits, servant in the house of the Divine King, and our admirable conductor, thou who dost shine with excellence and superhuman virtue, vouchsafe to deliver us from all evil, who turn to thee with confidence, and enable us by thy gracious protection to serve God more and more faithfully every day.

Pray for us, O glorious St. Michael, Prince of the Church of Jesus Christ.
That we may be made worthy of His promises.

Almighty and Everlasting God, who by a prodigy of goodness and a merciful desire for the salvation of all men, hast appointed the most glorious Archangel, St. Michael, Prince of Thy Church, make us worthy, we beseech Thee, to be delivered by his powerful protection from all our enemies, that none of them may harass us at the hour of death, but that we may be conducted by him into the august presence of Thy Divine Majesty. This we beg through the merits of Jesus Christ Our Lord. Amen.[31]

Indulgenced by Blessed Pope Pius IX
Imprimatur: Constantis, Feb. 1897, ABEL, Episc. Const. et Abr.

FIRST SATURDAY INVOCATIONS & PRAYERS

FATIMA SACRIFICE PRAYER:
Oh, my Jesus, I offer this for love of Thee, for the conversion of sinners, and in reparation for the sins committed against the Immaculate Heart of Mary.

FATIMA PARDON PRAYER:
My God, I believe, I adore, I trust, and I love Thee! I beg pardon for those who do not believe, do not adore, do not trust, and do not love Thee.

FATIMA ANGEL'S PRAYER:
O Most Holy Trinity – Father, Son and Holy Spirit – I adore Thee profoundly. I offer Thee the Most Precious Body, Blood, Soul, and Divinity of Jesus Christ, present in all the tabernacles of the world, in reparation for the outrages, sacrileges, and indifference by which He is offended. By the infinite merits of the Sacred Heart of Jesus, and the Immaculate Heart of Mary, I beg the conversion of poor sinners.

FATIMA EUCHARISTIC PRAYER:
Most Holy Trinity, I adore Thee! My God, My God, I love Thee in the most Blessed Sacrament.

PRAYER TO OUR LADY OF FATIMA:
Queen of the Rosary, Sweet Virgin of Fatima, who has deigned to appear in the land of Portugal, and has brought peace both interior and exterior, we beg of you, to watch over our dear homeland, and to assure its moral and spiritual revival. Bring back peace, to all nations of the world, so that all, and our own nation in particular, may be happy to call you their Queen of Peace.
Our Lady of the Rosary pray for our country.
Our Lady of Fatima, obtain for all humanity, a durable peace.
Amen.

THE FATIMA ROSARY DECADE PRAYER:
Oh, my Jesus, forgive us our sins, save us from the fires of hell, lead all souls to heaven, especially those in most need of Thy mercy.[32]

ANIMA CHRISTI PRAYER – said before or after receiving Communion
By St. Ignatius of Loyola

Soul of Christ, sanctify me;
Body of Christ, save me;
Blood of Christ, inebriate me;
Water from the side of Christ, wash me;
Passion of Christ, strengthen me;
O good Jesus, hear me;
within Your wounds, hide me;
separated from You let me never be;
from the evil one, protect me;
at the hour of my death, call me;
and close to You bid me;
that with Your saints, I may be
praising You forever and ever. Amen.

ACT OF CONSECRATION TO THE SACRED HEART

BY ST. MARGARET MARY ALACOQUE

O Sacred Heart of Jesus, to Thee I consecrate and offer up my person and my life, my actions, trials, and sufferings, that my entire being may henceforth only be employed in loving, honoring, and glorifying Thee. This is my irrevocable will, to belong entirely to Thee, and to do all for Thy love, renouncing with my whole heart all that can displease Thee.

I take Thee, O Sacred Heart, for the sole object of my love, the protection of my life, the pledge of my salvation, the remedy of my frailty and inconstancy, the reparation for all the defects of my life, and my secure refuge at the hour of my death. Be Thou, O Most Merciful Heart, my justification before God Thy Father, and screen me from His anger which I have so justly merited. I fear all from my own weakness and malice, but placing my entire confidence in Thee, O Heart of Love, I hope all from Thine infinite Goodness. Annihilate in me all that can displease or resist Thee. Imprint Thy pure love so deeply in my heart that I may never forget Thee or be separated from Thee.

I beseech Thee, through Thine infinite Goodness, grant that my name be engraved upon Thy Heart, for in this I place all my happiness and all my glory, to live and to die as one of Thy devoted servants. Amen.[33]

PRAYER TO THE SACRED HEART OF JESUS

O most holy heart of Jesus, fountain of every blessing, I adore you, I love you, and with lively sorrow for my sins I offer you this poor heart of mine. Make me humble, patient, pure and wholly obedient to your will. Grant, Good Jesus, that I may live in you and for you. Protect me in the midst of danger. Comfort me in my afflictions. Give me health of body, assistance in my temporal needs, thy blessing on all that I do, and the grace of a holy death. Within Thy Heart I place my every care. In every need let me come to Thee with humble trust saying, 'Heart of Jesus help me'. Amen.[34]

PRAYER FOR VOCATIONS BY ST. FAUSTINA

O my Jesus, I beg you on behalf of the whole Church:

Grant it love and the light of your Spirit, and give power to the words of priests so that hardened hearts might be brought to repentance and return to you, O Lord.

Lord, give us holy priests; you yourself maintain them in holiness.

O Divine and Great High Priest, may the power of your mercy accompany them everywhere and protect them from the devil's traps and snares which are continually being set for the souls of priests.

May the power of your mercy, O Lord, shatter and bring to naught all that might tarnish the sanctity of priests, for you can do all things. (Diary, 1052)

PADRE PIO'S FAVORITE PRAYER OF PETITION

Written by St. Margaret Mary Alacoque

*This prayer was said by St. Padre Pio when someone would ask him to pray for them. He has thousands of miracles associated with him, including the healing of Pope John Paul II. It is also called the "**Efficacious Novena to the Sacred Heart of Jesus**." It asks the Sacred Heart of Jesus to have mercy on us and our petitions.*

O my Jesus, You have said: "Truly I say to you, ask and you will receive, seek and you will find, knock and it will be opened to you." Behold I knock, I seek and ask for the grace of (here name your request). Our Father … Hail Mary … Glory Be … Sacred Heart of Jesus, I place all my trust in You.

O my Jesus, You have said: "Truly I say to you, if you ask anything of the Father in My name, He will give it to you." Behold, in Your name, I ask the Father for the grace of (here name your request). Our Father … Hail Mary … Glory Be … Sacred Heart of Jesus, I place all my trust in You.

O my Jesus, You have said: "Truly I say to you, heaven and earth will pass away but My words will not pass away." Encouraged by Your infallible words I now ask for the grace of (here name your request). Our Father … Hail Mary … Glory Be … Sacred Heart of Jesus, I place all my trust in You.

O Sacred Heart of Jesus, for whom it is impossible not to have compassion on the afflicted, have pity on us miserable sinners and grant us the grace which we ask of You, through the Sorrowful and Immaculate Heart of Mary, Your tender Mother and ours.

Say the Hail, Holy Queen (page 3) and end with: "St. Joseph, foster father of Jesus, pray for us." [35]

Artwork by Wendy Fluery

FLOS CARMELI PRAYER – *composed by St. Simon Stock. It is a prayer to the Blessed Virgin Mary, which has never been known to fail in obtaining her powerful help.*

O beautiful Flower of Carmel, most fruitful vine,
Splendor of Heaven, holy and singular,
who brought forth the Son of God,
still ever remaining a Pure Virgin,
assist me in this necessity.

O Star of the sea, help and protect me!
Show me that Thou art my Mother.

Strong stem of Jesse, who bore one
bright flower,
be ever near us, and guard us each hour,
who serve thee here.

Purest of lilies, that flowers among thorns,
bring help to true hearts that in weakness turn
and trust in thee.

Strongest of armour, we trust in thy might,
under thy mantle, hard pressed in the fight,
we call to thee.

Our way, uncertain, surrounded by foes,
unfailing counsel you offer to those
who turn to thee.

O gentle Mother, who in Carmel reigns,
share with your servants that gladness you gained,
and now enjoy.

Hail, gate of heaven, with glory now crowned,
bring us to safety, where thy Son is found,
true joy to see.

Holy Mary, Mother of Christ, hear the cry of your servants.
And bring down heavenly aid in answer to our prayer. [36]

END NOTES

15 Promises of the Rosary

[1] Mary Thierfelder, "Our Lady's 15 Promises to Those Who Pray Her Rosary," The Catholic Company, October 5, 2017, https://www.catholiccompany.com/magazine/15-promises-to-christians-who-pray-the-rosary-6146.

Divine Mercy

[2] Sister M. Faustina Kowalska, Diary: Divine Mercy in My Soul (Stockbridge, MA: Marian Press, 1987), 9. Hereafter cited internally.

Key Prayers

[3] "Ancient Prayer to St. Joseph," in The Original Pieta Prayer Booklet (Hickory Corners, MI: Miraculous Lady of the Roses, 2006), 19.

[4] "The Prayer of St. Gertrude the Great for the Souls in Purgatory," Scripture Catholic, accessed June 3, 2021, https://www.scripturecatholic.com/st-gertrude-prayer.

[5] The Council of Baltimore, Baltimore Catechism, No. 3, supplemented by Rev. Thomas L. Kinkead (Rockford, IL: Tan Books, 2010), 93.

[6] "Traditional Act of Faith, Hope & Charity in English & Latin," BeautySoAncient, August 17, 2020, https://www.beautysoancient.com/traditional-acts-of-faith-hope-charity-in-english-latin/.

Four Cardinal Virtues

[7] Catechism of the Catholic Church, 2nd ed. (Washington, DC: United States Catholic Conference, 1997), 443.

[8] "What is Virtue and What are the Four Cardinal Virtues?," Catholic Straight Answers, accessed May 14, 2021, https://catholicstraightanswers.com/what-is-virtue-and-what-are-the-four-cardinal-virtues/.

[9] Scott P. Richert, "What Are the 4 Cardinal Virtues?" Learn Religions, August 28, 2020, https://www.learnreligions.com/the-cardinal-virtues-542142.

Virtues versus Vices

[10] "Seven Virtues," Wikipedia, last modified April 20, 2021, https://en.wikipedia.org/wiki/Seven_virtues.

[11] St. Thomas Aquinas, "A Prayer for the Virtues," ed. Ben Myers, Faith & Theology, June 2, 2007, https://www.faith-theology.com/2007/06/prayer-for-virtues.html.

St. Andrew Christmas Novena

[12] Gretchen Filz, "St. Andrew's Christmas Novena Begins November 30," Catholic Company, November 29, 2016, https://www.catholiccompany.com/magazine/st-andrews-christmas-novena-november-30-5936.

The 7 Gifts of the Holy Spirit

[13] "Gifts of the Holy Spirit," Loyola Press, accessed March 8, 2021, https://www.loyolapress.com/catholic-resources/scripture-and-tradition/catholic-basics/catholic-beliefs-and-practices/gifts-of-the-holy-spirit.

[14] Frank X. Blisard, "The Seven Gifts of the Holy Spirit," Catholic Answers, June 10, 2019, https://www.catholic.com/magazine/print-edition/the-seven-gifts-of-the-holy-spirit.

The 12 Traditional Fruits of the Holy Spirit

[15] "The Twelve Fruits of the Holy Spirit," St. Catherine of Siena Catholic Church Faith Formation, accessed June 7, 2021, https://www.stcatfamilyfaith.com/uploads/4/0/5/2/4052266/the_twelve_fruits_of_the_holy_spirit_definitions.pdf.

The Seven Sacraments

[16] The Council of Baltimore, Baltimore Catechism, No. 3, 116.

[17] Fr. Lawrence Lovasik, SVD, The Seven Sacraments (New York: Catholic Book Publishing, 1962), 4.

[18] Lovasik, The Seven Sacraments, 3.

Reposition and Exposition

[19] "Rite of Eucharistic Exposition and Benediction: Exposition of the Blessed Sacrament," Diocese of Crookston Ministry Office, accessed July 15, 2021, https://www.crookston.org/documents/ministriesoffices/worship-a-liturgy/exposition-adoration/256-eucharistic-exposition-benediction/file.

Prayer of St. Francis of Assisi

[20] Fr. Kajetan Esser, OFM, "The Story Behind the Peace Prayer of St. Francis," Franciscan-Archive.org, accessed June 7, 2021, https://franciscan-archive.org/patriarcha/peace.html.

Prayers of the Mass

[21] Jeff Cavins, "The Parts of the Mass: The Confiteor," Ascension Press, September 25, 2019, https://media.ascensionpress.com/2019/09/25/the-parts-of-the-mass-the-confiteor/.

[22] Adrian Fortescue, "Confiteor – A General Confession of Sins," Catholic Answers, accessed March 8, 2021, https://www.catholic.com/encyclopedia/confiteor.

[23] "Parts of the Mass: The Gloria," St. Thomas the Apostle Catholic Church – Naperville, IL, accessed March 8, 2021, https://www.stapostle.org/explore-faith/parts-of-the-mass-the-gloria/.

[24] Lori Flanagan, "Explanation of the Mass - Introductory Rites, Gloria & Collect," SS. Edward & Isidore Blog, accessed March 8, 2021, https://www.stedwardisidore.org/blog/ss-edward-isidore-blog/explanation-of-the-mass-introductory-rites-gloria-collect.

[25] "The Meaning of the Nicene Creed: Why It's Still Relevant 17 Centuries Later," Daily Bread, accessed March 8, 2021, https://www.catholicfaithstore.com/daily-bread/meaning-nicene-creed/.

[26] "The Nicene Creed and its Origins," Catholic News Herald, July 28, 2016, https://catholicnewsherald.com/faith/101-news/faith/364-the-nicene-creed-and-its-origins.

[27] Pastor Stratman, "Sanctus/Holy, Holy, Holy," A Collection of Prayers, June 29, 2017, https://acolectionofprayers.com/2017/06/29/sanctus-holy-holy-holy/.

[28] Fr. Edward McNamara, "The Sanctus," EWTN, November 17, 2009, https://www.ewtn.com/catholicism/library/sanctus-4502.

The Golden Arrow Prayer

[29] "The Golden Arrow Prayer," America Needs Fatima, accessed June 15, 2021, https://www.americaneedsfatima.org/Our-Lord-Jesus-Christ/novena-to-the-holy-face-of-jesus.html.

Secrets Revealed to St. Faustina

[30] Billy Ryan, "When Jesus Revealed 25 Secrets of Spiritual Warfare in a Vision to Saint Faustina," uCatholic, November 11, 2019, https://ucatholic.com/blog/when-jesus-revealed-25-secrets-of-spiritual-warfare-in-a-vision-to-saint-faustina/.

Chaplet of Saint Michael

[31] "Chaplet of St. Michael," in The Original Pieta Prayer Booklet (Hickory Corners, MI: Miraculous Lady of the Roses, 2006), 70-73.

Immaculate Heart of Mary

[32] Blue Army of Our Lady of Fatima, First Saturday Devotions (Blue Island, IL: Blue Army of Our Lady of Fatima – Chicago Mother of Sorrow Complex, 2006).

Sacred Heart of Jesus

[33] St. Margaret Mary Alacoque, "Act of Consecration to the Sacred Heart," EWTN, accessed May 17, 2021, https://www.ewtn.com/catholicism/devotions/act-of-consecration-to-the-sacred-heart-12727.

[34] "Prayers to the Sacred Heart of Jesus," Traditional Catholic Prayers, October 8, 2019, https://traditionalcatholicprayers.com/2019/10/08/prayers-to-the-sacred-heart-of-jesus/.

[35] Attributed to St. Margaret Mary Alacoque, "Padre Pio's Favorite Prayer of Petition," Aleteia, accessed May 17, 2021, https://aleteia.org/2018/04/29/when-padre-pio-prayed-for-someone-he-used-this-powerful-prayer/.

Flos Carmeli Prayer & Alma Redemptoris Mater

[36] 13th century hymn attributed to Simon Stock, "The Flos Carmeli," The British Province of Carmelites, accessed May 17, 2021, https://www.carmelite.org/carmelite-spirituality/prayer-carmel/flos-carmeli.

Bibliography

The Rosary

Thierfelder, Mary. "Our Lady's 15 Promises to Those Who Pray Her Rosary." The Catholic Company. October 5, 2017. https://www.catholiccompany.com/magazine/15-promises-to-christians-who-pray-the-rosary-6146.

Divine Mercy

Kowalska, Saint Maria Faustina. Diary: Divine Mercy in My Soul. Stockbridge, MA: Marian Press, 1987.

Key Prayers

"Ancient Prayer to St. Joseph." In The Original Pieta Prayer Booklet. Hickory Corners, MI: Miraculous Lady of the Roses, 2006.

BeautySoAncient. "Traditional Act of Faith, Hope & Charity in English & Latin." August 17, 2020. https://www.beautysoancient.com/traditional-acts-of-faith-hope-charity-in-english-latin/.

Scripture Catholic. "The Prayer of St. Gertrude the Great for the Souls in Purgatory." Accessed June 3, 2021. https://www.scripturecatholic.com/st-gertrude-prayer.

The Council of Baltimore. Baltimore Catechism, No. 3. Supplemented by Rev. Thomas L. Kinkead. Rockford, IL: Tan Books, 2010.

Four Cardinal Virtues

Catechism of the Catholic Church, 2nd ed. Washington, DC: United States Catholic Conference, 1997.

Catholic Straight Answers. "What is virtue and what are the four cardinal virtues?. Accessed May 14, 2021. https://catholicstraightanswers.com/what-is-virtue-and-what-are-the-four-cardinal-virtues/.

Richert, Scott P. "What Are the 4 Cardinal Virtues?." Learn Religions. August 28, 2020. https://www.learnreligions.com/the-cardinal-virtues-542142.

Virtues versus Vices

Myers, Ben. "A Prayer for the Virtues." Faith & Theology. June 2, 2017. https://www.faith-theology.com/2007/06/prayer-for-virtues.html.

Wikipedia. "Seven Virtues." Last modified April 20, 2021. https://en.wikipedia.org/wiki/Seven_virtues.

St. Andrew Christmas Novena

Filz, Gretchen. "St. Andrew's Christmas Novena Begins November 30." Catholic Company. Accessed November 29, 2016. https://www.catholiccompany.com/magazine/st-andrews-christmas-novena-november-30-5936.

Seven Gifts of the Holy Spirit

Blisard, Frank X. "The Seven Gifts of the Holy Spirit." Catholic Answers. June 10, 2019. https://www.catholic.com/magazine/print-edition/the-seven-gifts-of-the-holy-spirit.

Loyola Press. "Gifts of the Holy Spirit." Accessed March 8, 2021. https://www.loyolapress.com/catholic-resources/scripture-and-tradition/catholic-basics/catholic-beliefs-and-practices/gifts-of-the-holy-spirit/.

RCL Benziger. "Sacraments." Accessed March 8, 2021. http://rclbsacraments.com/confirmation/confirmation-gifts-fruits-holy-spirit.

Traditional Catholic. "Lesson Sixteenth: On the Gifts & Fruits of the Holy Spirit." In Traditional Catholic Baltimore Catechism #2. Accessed March 8, 2021. http://traditionalcatholic.net/Tradition/Information/Baltimore_No-2.html#Lesson%2016.

Van Sloun, Rev. Michael A. "What are the Seven Gifts of the Holy Spirit." Archdiocese of St. Paul & Minneapolis. Accessed March 8, 2021. https://www.archspm.org/faith-and-discipleship/catholic-faith/what-are-the-seven-gifts-of-the-holy-spirit/.

The 12 Traditional Fruits of the Holy Spirit

St. Catherine of Siena Catholic Church Faith Formation. "The Twelve Fruits of the Holy Spirit." Accessed June 7, 2021. https://www.stcatfamilyfaith.com/uploads/4/0/5/2/4052266/the_twelve_fruits_of_the_holy_spirit_definitions.pdf.

The Seven Sacraments

Lovasik Fr. Lawrence, S.V.D. The Seven Sacraments. New York: Catholic Book Publishing, 1962.

Reposition and Exposition

Diocese of Crookston Ministry Office. "Rite of Eucharistic Exposition and Benediction: Exposition of the Blessed Sacrament." Accessed July 15, 2021. https://www.crookston.org/documents/ministriesoffices/worship-a-liturgy/exposition-adoration/256-eucharistic-exposition-benediction/file.

Prayer of St. Francis of Assisi

Esser, Fr. Kajetan, OFM. "The Story Behind the Peace Prayer of St. Francis." Franciscan Archive. Accessed June 7, 2021. https://www.franciscan-archive.org/patriarcha/peace.htm.

Prayers of the Mass

Catholic News Herald. "The Nicene Creed and its origins." July 28, 2016. https://catholicnewsherald.com/faith/101-news/faith/364-the-nicene-creed-and-its-origins.

Cavins, Jeff. "The Parts of the Mass: The Confiteor." Ascension Press. September 25, 2019. https://media.ascensionpress.com/2019/09/25/the-parts-of-the-mass-the-confiteor/.

Daily Bread. "The Meaning of the Nicene Creed: Why It's Still Relevant 17 Centuries later." Accessed March 8, 2021. https://www.catholicfaithstore.com/daily-bread/meaning-nicene-creed/.

Fortescue, Adrian. "Confiteor – A general confession of sins." Catholic Answers. Accessed March 8, 2021. https://www.catholic.com/encyclopedia/confiteor.

Flanagan, Lori. "Explanation of the Mass-Introductory Rites-Gloria & Collect." SS. Edward & Isidore Blog. Accessed March 8, 2021. https://www.stedwardisidore.org/blog/ss-edward-isidore-blog/explanation-of-the-mass-introductory-rites-gloria-collect.

McNamara, Fr. Edward. "The Sanctus." EWTN. November 17, 2009. Accessed May 15, 2021 https://www.ewtn.com/catholicism/library/sanctus-4502.

Stratman. "Sanctus/Holy, Holy, Holy." A Collection of Prayers. June 29, 2017. https://acolectionofprayers.com/2017/06/29/sanctus-holy-holy-holy/.

St. Thomas the Apostle Catholic Church – Naperville, IL. "Parts of the Mass: The Gloria." Accessed March 8, 2021. https://www.stapostle.org/explore-faith/parts-of-the-mass-the-gloria/.

The Golden Arrow Prayer

America Needs Fatima. "The Golden Arrow Prayer." Accessed June 15, 2021. https://www.americaneedsfatima.org/Our-Lord-Jesus-Christ/novena-to-the-holy-face-of-jesus.html.

Secrets Revealed to St. Faustina

Ryan, Billy. "When Jesus Revealed 25 Secrets of Spiritual Warfare in a Vision to Saint Faustina." uCatholic. November 11, 2019. https://ucatholic.com/blog/when-jesus-revealed-25-secrets-of-spiritual-warfare-in-a-vision-to-saint-faustina/.

Chaplet of St. Michael

"Chaplet of St. Michael" In The Original Pieta Prayer Booklet. Hickory Corners, MI: Miraculous Lady of the Roses, 2006.

The Immaculate Heart of Mary

Blue Army of Our Lady of Fatima. First Saturday Devotions. Blue Island, IL: Blue Army of Our Lady of Fatima – Chicago Mother of Sorrow Complex, 2006.

The Sacred Heart of Jesus

Alacoque, St. Margaret Mary. "Act of Consecration to the Sacred Heart." EWTN. Accessed May 17, 2021. https://www.ewtn.com/catholicism/devotions/act-of-consecration-to-the-sacred-heart-12727.

Traditional Catholic Prayers. "Prayers to the Sacred Heart of Jesus." October 8, 2019. https://traditionalcatholicprayers.com/2019/10/08/prayers-to-the-sacred-heart-of-jesus/.

Attributed to St. Margaret Mary Alacoque. "Padre Pio's favorite Prayer of Petition." Aleteia. Accessed May 17, 2021. https://aleteia.org/2018/04/29/when-padre-pio-prayed-for-someone-he-used-this-powerful-prayer/.

13th century hymn attributed to Simon Stock. "Alma Redemptoris Mater: Loving Mother of the Redeemer." The Mary Foundation. Accessed May 17, 2021. https://www.catholicity.com/prayer/alma-redempto ries-ma ter-loving-mother-of-the-redeemer.html.

Duoay-Rheims Bible. Accessed April 30, 2021. http://drbo.org/about.htm.